The Prosperity Mentor: Elevating Your Financial Success

Denny M. Gowan

INTRODUCTION

Close your eyes and picture a magical trip, a winding path studded with the gems of financial wealth, a hidden path leading to a life infused with the enchantment of riches. Imagine a mentor at this point—a wealthy wizard who not only knows the way to the mystic goal but can also lead you through all of its magical wonders. Give us the chance to introduce you to "The Prosperity Mentor."

The Prosperity Mentor stands out as a mystical sage, a sorcerer of success, and a conjurer of change in a world where financial fortunes fluctuate like tides and where the chase of money may be as elusive as chasing a rainbow's end.

Throughout history, mentors have served as the enchanted keepers of the secrets of greatness, guarding everything from the profound knowledge of ancient philosophers to the modern-day spells conjured by entrepreneurial geniuses. Although they come from this mystical lineage, The Prosperity Mentor are experts in riches, success, and the art of flourishing.

Imagine this as your invitation to set off on an exciting journey, helped by a wise tutor who is familiar with the secret spells for achieving financial success. The Prosperity Mentor is more than just a teacher of wealth creation; they hold the alchemical secrets to a life in which money worries become untrue fairy tales and prosperity becomes your reliable friend.

Prepare to reveal hidden scrolls, decipher strong spells, and embrace transforming incantations as we explore deeper into the enchanted world of The Prosperity Mentor. These will take you to a place of financial plenty that you previously thought only existed in dreams. This mentor, a renowned figure in the field of plenty, is prepared to provide the esoteric knowledge and mystical direction necessary to help you reach your greatest potential.

So be ready for a fantastical voyage where you'll discover not only how to make riches but also how to preserve it, as well as—most importantly—how to live a life that thrives and prospers in every dimension. Welcome to "The Prosperity Mentor's world, where your financial future is going to take on a magical change and the road to wealth awaits, brimming with wonders beyond your wildest dreams.

The Prosperity Mentor is a singular mix of money know-how and artistic alchemy. They are about building a tapestry of success that touches every area of your life, not just about counting dollars and cents. Their advice goes beyond the ordinary, kindling a flame of creativity and enchantment on your path to financial security.

The core of The Prosperity Mentor is built on knowledge, refined throughout time by experience, and adorned with the gems of original thought. They have a financial magic wand, making them the modern-day equal of

Merlin. Their wealth is a real, attainable truth; it is not an ephemeral illusion.

The Prosperity Mentor is the keeper of the golden thread amid the maze of financial difficulties. They have a remarkable gift for boiling down complicated ideas into workable concoctions, turning wealth creation into a doable kind of art. They serve as your compass as you navigate the confusing world of investing choices, risk management, and asset protection. You may handle the financial world with confidence and composure under their direction.

But The wealth Mentor's enchantment goes well beyond merely material wealth. It includes people's whole well-being, where money isn't just a figure on a balance sheet but also a source of fulfillment, joy, and the ability to have a major effect. It's about striking that elusive work-life balance and enjoying an abundant life that includes your connections with others, your health, and your sense of purpose.

The knowledge of this mentor is not limited by age, work, or financial status. They serve as a mentor for those who are interested in learning, aspiring entrepreneurs, seasoned workers, and retirees looking for financial security. Anyone who is ready to dream big, rewrite their financial history, and change their lives via the power of wealth can learn from them.

You're in for a life-changing journey if you're prepared to set off on a mythological quest for financial mastery under the tutelage of The Prosperity Mentor.Put your seatbelt on, let the unusual enter your mind, and allow the alchemy of prosperity to carry you to realms you've only dared to dream of. Here, with the promise of financial enchantment and a life that actually prospers in every way, your journey starts

Chapter 1

what is a Monetization models

A monetization model is a strategy (or a method) for making money out of a product, service, piece of intellectual property, or even your own brand. Your monetization strategy may include a variety of components, but for you to make the required profit, they all need to work together.

For example, you might choose to charge for downloads, include advertisements, or combine all three when creating an app. Or, if you were a software developer, you might choose from a number of monetization methods. You could grant customers the right to "white label" it and use it along with their own branding. You can either sell access under your own brand or offer free access with a "freemium" upgrade.

A monetization model explains how several revenue streams, whether they are numerous or few, are integrated to produce a brand's overall revenue.

many monetization strategies

These are a few of the common ways to monetize. However, these are not the only revenue streams. In the end, new ways to monetize are constantly being developed. Keep in mind that these are not mutually exclusive, and that many brands utilize more than one of them (with some overlap).

1.Member monetization: Member-led growth is one of the highest forms of monetization. Those companies that can convert customers, users, and subscribers into subscribers will be part of the next wave of rapidly expanding industries. And they'll do it in large quantities.

The technique of member-led monetization may be as simple as assessing a membership fee to a community. But doing so produces valuable ongoing income, AND members of your community create content and spread the word, enabling growth on autopilot.

Some examples of member-led monetization in action are as follows:

• A commercial entity. I released a branded app for 5,000 subscribers, and in just over two weeks, I made over $30,000.

•A launch to 100 high-ticket members that focused on health had an increase in ARR of $40,000.

•An author and public speaker increased their sales by $30,000 during a four-week promotion they launched in their membership community.

•In just two months, one community that offered a 13-week add-on course generated an additional $100k in revenue.In just ten days, a podcaster and novelist sold 5,000 seats for a $997 course to subscribers.

You'll find that when you have a member-based product, you frequently profit from both the membership fees and the add-ons that members buy—a business model McKinsey refers to as a community flywheel.

2.Digital Subscriptions : Although your subscribers don't make any contributions, subscription-based monetization works very similarly to the member model. Instead, they make use of tools or content that you have either licensed or generated yourself. Because companies like Microsoft and Dropbox mainly rely on subscription revenue, it's a popular business model for software companies.

It also holds true for content; businesses like Netflix and Disney have prospered thanks to subscription services. In 2020, when there were 8 million print and digital subscribers, even the New York Times was kept afloat by subscriptions.

3.Freemium: Software firms appreciate the freemium monetization model since it enables users to try a product for free before committing. Since there is no upfront payment necessary, the monetization structure in this case handles the free trial, which does away with the requirement for "money back guarantees" and the like. In addition, it makes it easier for users, subscribers, etc. to upgrade in order to either access more features or skip the paywall sooner.

4.Product-led monetization: On occasion, a product might serve as the best monetization strategy. It might be something digital, like a top-tier online course. For instance, as we said above, a podcaster and author on Mighty sold 5,000 seats for a $997 course in just 10 days. It makes sense to monetize digital things in this way.

However, selling tangible items is also a tried-and-true way to make money, and there are some seriously cool companies who have figured out how to convert internet buzz into real-world sales success.

Consider Peloton, which created a real-world bike that linked users to other fitness fanatics and exercise routines in real time. Peleton's maturity during the pandemic, when people were searching for exercises to do, was also advantageous. Famous people have also used their brands to publicize the launching of actual products. Ryan Reynolds, who recently sold his Aviation Gin company for $610 million, is one such instance.

The integration of items with online attention is still in its early stages, so we'll see a lot more of it in the future.

5.Licensing: For people who own any form of intellectual property, licensing can be a terrific way to make money. It is an underestimated technique of revenue production. Owning a specific method or model and selling the right to use it to others is the essence of licensing. If you come across someone selling the "Trademarked

X method to X," you're most likely looking at a license agreement.

For instance, many thought leaders build their identities through venues like TED Talks and op-eds before granting permission for companies to adopt their ideas.

How to draft a monetization strategy

Here are some ideas to aid you in developing your plan as you are ready to monetize:

1. Recognize your advantages: Many attempts at monetization fail due to a lack of brand knowledge. Think about a situation when you have a few loyal followers. Ads can be the least profitable kind of monetization because they demand a lot of volume. The ideal product can be one that is customized. On the other hand, if your website had a vast viewership and no clear niche, adverts might make more sense. A product is unlikely to prosper without a clear niche. Find your strengths and select the model that best matches them.

2. Talk to your present team. Consult your present members to find out what they most desire from you if you're thinking about creating a product or service to monetize. This is as simple to do in an online community as a poll.

3. Verify that it works: A lot of monetization attempts fail because the target market isn't understood. One example is a story about a blogger who offered advice to young people looking for work on how to introduce a pricy product. It was utterly unsuccessful. Although the audience was enthusiastic, many lacked money because they were out of work.

4. Take note of the business-related elements: The IRS has some strong opinions about making money, even if it is done online. Ensure that you are familiar with the income claim procedure. Visit your local small business center; they can typically show you what you need. This can be an excellent suggestion.

5.Adapt, test, and learn: Your initial method of monetization might not be the ideal one. Until you discover what works best for you and your audience, don't be scared to try various things (and let things go).

Chapter 2

How to scale a product

In this article, scaling tactics for digital products are discussed, with a focus on product-market fit, customer experience, development procedures, and flexible business operations.

A digital business' success depends on the concept of scaling a product. It speaks to a product's ability to handle increasing workloads effectively and economically. Enhancing a product's functionality and ensuring that it can accommodate a surge in additional consumers without sacrificing the caliber of the customer experience are the two main objectives of scaling a product. However, the product manager and the development team must put up more work and considerable development to achieve this goal.

1. The Importance of Product Market Fit: Achieving product market fit is crucial before growing a product. This phrase signifies that a product is in demand and that it satisfies the needs of a particular market niche. Any attempts at rapid scaling are likely to fail without obtaining product-market fit. It is simpler to concentrate on scaling your product if a concept has shown to have a large market fit. After that, your development team should focus on expanding the product's functionality and getting it ready for scale.

Achieving product-market fit is a continuous process, so keep that in mind. New features must be continuously integrated based on market trends and client input. It is crucial to keep a careful eye on market trends and consumer needs because as your product scales, the product market fit may change.

2. Empowering the Development Team: A product's scaling depends heavily on the development team. The group is in charge of creating software and making sure the process of creating digital products is carried out successfully. The development team puts in a lot of effort to make sure the product is prepared for scaling, starting with the creation of the minimum viable product (MVP) and continuing with revisions depending on customer input.

The use of continuous integration and quality assurance techniques is another key component for the development team. These procedures are essential to software development since they make sure the final product is error-free and operates at its best. This is crucial when working with mobile apps because poor performance can negatively affect user experience.

3. Creating a Solid Marketing Plan: The success of your product depends on how many people know about it and value it. As a result, developing a solid marketing plan requires time and money when scaling a product. Reaching new customers, boosting product functionality, and providing an exceptional customer experience should be the main goals of this strategy.

4. Simplifying Business Operations: Scaling a product involves more than just the software development team and the development team itself. It also affects numerous business sectors and calls for adjustments to how businesses operate. To manage the influx of new customers and to enable the quick scaling of your product, all business operations—from sales and marketing efforts to customer service and finance—should be streamlined.

Adopting new technology can be quite beneficial in this regard. Automation and AI, for instance, can expedite processes and free up resources to concentrate on more critical duties.

5.Slow vs. quick Scaling: It's a widely held belief that quick scaling is the best success statistic. Fast product scaling, nevertheless, can occasionally backfire. Slow scaling enables the product manager and development team to prioritize quality control and iteratively enhance the product in response to user input.

Fast scale dealing, in comparison, may bring in a sizable number of new consumers, but it also presents a number of difficulties, including handling a higher need for customer service while preserving product quality and customer happiness. As a result, it's crucial to balance gradual scaling and fast scaling according to the market and the preparedness of your product.

How to leverage product diversity to distinguish yourself from your rivals

It is exceedingly challenging to remain relevant in a highly competitive market.
in particular when "brand diversity" is not being used as it should. For this reason, a lot of companies view product diversity as an effective growth tactic.

Basically, having a well-defined development and growth strategy enables you to seek new options or possibilities to expand the brand's market presence, boost sales, boost profits, and stabilize corporate earnings.

We'll go into more detail about product diversity in this article. For instance, the various forms of diversification, their importance, their advantages, and perhaps even how a small brand can diversify. To help you better comprehend this tactic, we'll walk you through a few examples of product diversification.

Exactly why do brands diversify?

Diversification has numerous benefits, but one of the most important is to stand out from the crowd. It also helps to resolve several issues, including:

•Survival — Businesses can use diversification tactics to promote new sales of specific items when sales of such products are declining.

•Adapting to change — It only makes sense to diversify your business in light of social changes that affect consumer demand and behavior as well as recent advancements in research and technology.

•A desire to grow into a new or larger market; for a small business trying to grow, diversifying its product offerings is a fantastic method to do so.

•Avoiding overspecialization, which can prevent an organization's expansion by forcing it to sell only in a single market. Introducing new products can be a terrific approach to leave the realm of specialty.

strategies to diversify in order to outperform the competition

The most popular tactics or strategies for diversity are:

1. Extension: Adding new features to an existing product line enables you to release a new iteration of the same range of goods. For instance, if you sell energy nut bits with almonds as the primary component and there are already four flavors available on the market, such as almond, hazelnut, pistachio, and coconut, you can add a fifth flavor, like cashew. The fresh taste serves as an additional feature or element in this kind of scenario to draw in a new target market. The cashew nut energy bite will then join the family of products as a new sibling.

2. Renaming: Renaming your products is a diversification approach that might be useful if you want to enter a foreign market. With a new name for the new market, you can offer a product that is exactly the same as the original one in the existing market. For instance, if you currently sell flower bouquets under a brand that has cultural connotations specific to your present market, you may rename it to reflect the culture of the potential new market. Essentially, to adapt the product to the target market. However, if you're targeting the worldwide market, say by selling on an online marketplace, you might need to give the product a generic name that people from all cultures can relate to.

3. Repackaging: is an additional method of product diversification. In this case, you merely offer your products a new, improved package, similar to renaming. When you consider that 72% of customers' purchasing decisions are influenced by packaging designs, a small modification could open up a new market for you. You can alter the appearance of your bottles or containers if you sell hair or skincare products, for instance. Consumers are becoming more and more concerned about how packaging affects the environment today. Therefore, by diversifying your business, you can draw in a new group of customers if you look into sustainable packaging.
One business that employs ecological packaging is Waitrose.

4. Resizing: is the process of changing an existing product's size or quantity so that it can satisfy the demands of a different market. You can adjust the quantity to sell a product in a unit of 10 if you sell it in just one, or the other way around. There are several inventive possibilities with regard to sizing. For instance, you may introduce the product in a travel size.

5. Repricing: is another way to diversify your product offerings by changing the price of your goods. For instance, you can alter the manufacturing process for expensive or high-end goods and
Sell for more money. Alternatively, if you want to reduce the cost, you might use different materials and charge.

Chapter 3

Productivity and growth

Growth and productivity are two crucial elements of both economic and psychological development. They are interrelated and significantly influence the prosperity of people, companies, and entire economies.

Productivity is the effectiveness with which inputs, like labor, capital, and technology, are converted into outputs, like commodities and services. Making the most of your time and resources to accomplish your goals is important in a personal setting. Because they can produce more with less resources, companies with higher productivity typically have higher profitability.

Contrarily, growth generally refers to an expansion in an entity's capacity, size, or scale, whether it be a corporation, an economy, or a person's personal development. Personal growth entails increasing one's knowledge, abilities, and experiences while economic progress is gauged by indicators like the Gross Domestic Product (GDP).

Productivity and growth are closely related in the following ways:

Economic expansion is mostly fueled by productivity. A nation or business may produce more goods and services with the same resources as it becomes more productive, which raises GDP and raises living standards.

•**Technology and innovation**: Productivity gains are frequently a result of technological developments and innovations. These developments can stimulate economic expansion and open up new options for both people and enterprises.

•**Personal Development**: Increasing productivity is essential for developing oneself. Effective time management, setting and achieving objectives, and skill improvement are all components of personal productivity that support personal development.

Productivity is an important component of corporate success. Businesses with high levels of productivity can provide customers competitive prices, superior quality, and innovation, which expands their market share and profits.

•**Quality of Life:** People may have a higher quality of life as a result of increased productivity. People would have more free time, better living circumstances, and access to a greater variety of goods and services if resources were used more effectively.

•**Sustainability**: Using resources wisely and reducing adverse effects on the environment are necessary for sustainable productivity and growth. For economies and people to thrive in the long run, sustainable growth is essential.

In conclusion, productivity and growth are related ideas that affect one another. Economic and personal progress can be fueled by higher productivity, while growth itself can open up chances for higher productivity. For an organization to be successful and sustainable over the long run, these two factors must be balanced. The quest for productivity and growth is an ongoing process of growth and development, both personally and economically.

Success necessitates productivity.

Absolutely, success and productivity are sometimes tightly related. The ability to use one's resources, such as time, effort, and abilities, effectively and efficiently is known as productivity. Here are some examples of how productivity is essential for success:

•**Achieving Goals**: Productivity aids in the accomplishment of goals and objectives for both individuals and enterprises. You can move steadily closer to your goals by successfully managing time and resources.

•**Time Management**: Successful people frequently possess the ability to use their time effectively. Their productivity is increased because they prioritize activities, cut off distractions, and pay attention to what matters most.

•**Consistency**: To be productive, one must not only work hard but also consistently. Small, persistent efforts over time are typically the key to success, and this can only be done through productivity.

•**Efficiency**: Getting more done in less time is a sign of productivity. This effectiveness can provide one a competitive edge in both professional and personal endeavors.

•**Adaptability**: People who are very productive are frequently better at adjusting to new situations and difficulties. Even when faced with unforeseen obstacles, they are able to alter their strategies, keep organized, and stay focused.

•**Innovation**: By fostering productivity, innovation can flourish. You have greater mental capacity to think creatively and generate fresh ideas when you're effectively managing your chores.

•**Work-Life Balance**: Achieving a better work-life balance, which is essential for personal achievement, can also be facilitated by productivity. You can have more time for leisure activities and relaxation if your work is completed quickly.

•**Positive Habits**: Creating positive habits is important for productivity. Success is a sequence of accomplishments built on reliable, productive habits rather than a single feat.

•**Learning and Growth**: Highly productive people frequently pursue personal growth and learning opportunities. They invest time in learning new things, which can greatly increase their chances of success.

•**Professional Success**: Those who consistently create results and demonstrate productivity at work are more likely to advance in their careers, be promoted, and have a prosperous professional life.

Productivity, in essence, is the engine that powers the success-oriented vehicle. While the idea of success varies from person to person, productivity is a universal ability that can help individuals and organizations achieve their different definitions of success. Making the most of your resources, setting and pursuing goals, and maintaining a growth mindset are all critical components. Productivity is an important ally on the journey, whether you're attempting to achieve at work, in your personal life, or in any other area.

What exactly is a strategic planning consultant?

Strategic planning necessitates that businesses consider the long term and establish their top goals for the next year or two. Rather than focusing on a specific product or business unit, this type of planning assesses a complete organization and its progress toward a goal. Momentum provides strategic planning services to small businesses, healthcare organizations, and government agencies.

Professional strategic planning services

The methods in which strategic planning can aid a company vary based on its current situation. The aims of the exercise, the age of the organization, and the industry in which it competes all have an impact on the breadth and character of these services. These considerations can influence meeting frequency; for example, organizations in rapidly changing fields may need to convene these types of planning sessions twice a year.

These strategic planning consultation sessions are often divided into three parts:

•**Assessment**: The best way to start the strategic planning process is to determine how a business currently runs, analyzing every aspect of the business.

•**Planning**: The goal-setting step of the process in which the business's vision is established, taking information from the assessment stage into specific consideration.

•**Execution**: Using the information gathered during the evaluation and planning meetings, a quantifiable and practical strategy is developed.

Momentum can aid businesses in successfully preparing for the future and working toward attainable goals.

Benefits of momentum's strategic planning services

Momentum's strategic planning strategy supports firms in determining their goals and initiating major effort toward realizing them. Businesses can benefit from our comprehensive technique in the following ways.

•**Defined Goals:** When a company's purpose is clearly articulated, it is easier to create goals and objectives to fulfill it. This enables businesses to set implementation timelines and ensure that their resources are invested in a way that will eventually benefit the firm.

•**Better Communication**: By having clearly stated goals, organizations may lay the groundwork for their employees to understand. Employees can work with concrete targets that are easy to quantify and understand rather than foggy concepts and ambiguous goals. It also acts as a framework for performance appraisals, which can motivate employees to work more and create more. Inform the stakeholders about the organization's goals and objectives.

•**Increased Satisfaction**: The strategic planning process considers everyone's viewpoints while determining an organization's status and objectives. Once completed, it provides everyone involved with clear goals to work toward. These two factors significantly increase employee happiness because they provide employees with a better sense of agency and participation within the firm.

Momentum's high-quality materials and best-practice solutions increase these benefits. Momentum guarantees unique solutions for each company through tailored, hands-on tactics that produce the best results in the short and long term.

Chapter 4

what is mass customization

The art of mass customisation entails designing goods that naturally adapt to their surroundings or using packaging, marketing, or cosmetics to best match the needs of each unique buyer. Customers respond more positively to mass customisation, which also provides businesses with the freedom and connectivity needed to create personalized goods at reduced prices for mass production.

Innovative production methods and technologies, often known as made-to-order or built-to-order, were created to allow companies to make replaceable parts that customers can select from. A sectional couch or sofa, for instance, might be offered by a furniture maker with a variety of configuration choices and options for legs, fabrics, and colors so that a buyer can fit it to their sitting area.

Many businesses, including the following, use mass customization:

Software for computers: Developers of software employ mass customisation to combine product settings and add-ons that clients choose to change particular functions of a core product.

Financial: Independent advice companies allow you to spread your holdings, choose products that fit your investment risk tolerance, investing style, time outlook, and future goals by mass customizing them.

Retail: You can build a modular home using base packages or upgrades, much as you can personalize a car using its features and choices. A suit shop gives you options for colors and materials, and then tailors it for you with your choice of buttons and stitches. Even a flower shop can add beloved flowers to a design or bouquet.

While retaining the benefits of mass production's cheaper costs, mass customization supports strong product sales and high customer satisfaction ratings.

How marketing uses mass tailoring

In order to gain a competitive edge over competing companies or those that only offer generic items, organizations use mass customization in their marketing efforts. The key is letting buyers know they can make certain product components through a mix-and-match or made-to-order choice. A customer may build a better sense of brand loyalty as a result of this.

Companies can: By touting the availability of cheap product customization without losing quality, they can:

Gain competitive edge, connect customers, keep prices at mass production levels, produce more profit, be seen as flexible, and increase sales.

In order to watch or hear advertising messages that are specifically targeted to a user as a particular market group or with messages you know they appreciate, companies can utilize mass customisation as a marketing technique.

Four different kinds of mass customization

The following are the four main types of mass customization:

1.Collaborative: Businesses partner with customers to provide goods or services that are especially suited to them, such as a pizza shop that offers a range of pizza toppings.

2. Adaptive: Businesses build goods that are standardized but that the customer may adjust. An example of this would be giving a flexible pocket knife that the customer can use whatever they see fit.

3. Cosmetics: Businesses make similar things but market them to different groups in different ways, such as a store brand ice cream made and sold by a luxury brand producer.

4. Transparent: Businesses offer distinctive products to specific customers without making it clear that the products are customized, for example by using a product recommendation tool on online shops or in sales letters sent to customers.

Mass customization benefits

Utilizing mass tailoring in production, advertising, and sales has a number of benefits, including:

•**Efficiency of production**: Mass customisation allows firms to continue manufacturing in huge quantities, frequently with product differentiation happening only in the last stage to control costs while keeping customization.

•**Sale influence**: Customers who choose parts of their purchases through mass tailoring may be more likely to choose one company over another when making a purchase.

•**Higher revenue**: Mass customisation allows a seller, maker, or business to successfully demand a higher price and increase sales revenue.

• **Cost savings**: Mass customization lowers costs by weighing the time and resources needed for mass production against the high cost of individually created items. It also helps handle longer inventory costs involved with storing unique things.

Chapter 5

Effective contract and Proposal

Organizations and individuals may set clear agreements, norms, and conditions for a particular project or transaction with the use of effective contracts and plans. These documents aid in preventing misunderstandings, safeguarding the interests of all parties, and guaranteeing the smooth functioning of the activity or collaboration. Here are some crucial factors to take into account while writing strong contracts and proposals:

Effective Proposals:

Use simple, unambiguous language that is easy to understand when describing your plan. To avoid confusing the reader, avoid using jargon or excessively technical terminology.

Clearly define the work or services to be rendered in the detailed scope of work. Make sure there are no misunderstandings by outlining what is and is not included.

Pricing and Payment Terms: Offer a thorough cost analysis that takes into account all factors and contingencies. Make payment conditions, including when and how money is due, clear.

Include a project plan with key objectives and completion dates. This helps to manage expectations and makes sure that everyone is aware of the expected arrival times.

•Qualifications and Experience: Make sure to highlight your training, pertinent work experience, and application expertise. Describe why you and your group are the most qualified applicants for the post.

•Client Advantages Describe how the client will benefit from your plan. How will your offerings meet their requirements and solve their issues?

•References and Case Studies: To show your successful track record, provide references or case studies, if they are accessible.

•Describe any terms and conditions that apply to your plan in your statement of terms. Examples of this include warranties, intellectual property rights, and responsibility provisions.

•Customization: Tailor your offer to the particular interests and aspirations of the consumer. A one-size-fits-all approach has a lower likelihood of success.

•Professional Formatting: Ensure that your plan is well-structured, free of errors, and written in a professional manner. A well-done performance could leave an excellent impression.

Successful agreements:

•Parties and Signatories: Clearly include the names, titles, and contact information of all contract parties. Name the signatory power holders for the contract.

•Specify the range of the labor or the goods/services that will be offered. Include guidelines, benchmarks, and any other relevant technical data.

•Payment terms: Clearly state the terms of payment, including the amount, deadlines, and any late payment fees. Specify the payment method, such as a bank transfer, check, or online transaction.

•Duration and Termination: Clearly state the length of the agreement, as well as the conditions under which either party may terminate it.

Discuss intellectual property rights ownership, in particular who owns any creative works or •information.

•Describe the process for making and accepting contract revisions and amendments.

•Execution and signatures: Ensure that all parties sign the agreement and retain copies for their keeping.

Easiest ways to make contracts and proposal to work

Making contracts and proposals operate successfully demands clear communication, mutual understanding, and a commitment to honoring the agreed-upon parameters. Here are some of the easiest ways to ensuring contracts and proposals perform as intended:

For Proposals:

•**comprehend Client Needs**: Before producing a proposal, completely comprehend the client's needs, preferences, and objectives. Tailor your proposal to suit their individual requirements.

•**Clear and Concise Language**: Use straightforward language in your proposal to guarantee clarity. Avoid jargon or too technical terminology that can confuse the client.

•**Detailed Scope of Work**: Clearly explain the scope of the project or services to be offered. Be precise about what is included and what is not.

•**prices Transparency**: Provide a thorough breakdown of expenses and prices. Make sure your price is straightforward and easy to grasp.

•**Realistic Timelines**: Ensure that the planned timetable and milestones are realistic and doable. Unrealistic timelines might lead to complications later.

•**Professional Presentation**: Present your proposal in a professional and well-organized way. A flawless presentation may make a great impression.

•**Follow-Up:** After submitting the proposal, follow up with the customer to answer any questions or concerns. A personal touch may go a long way.

•**customer Benefits**: Clearly outline the benefits the customer will gain from your proposal. How will your services or product fulfill their demands and give value?

For contracts:

•**Clear and thorough wording**: Ensure that the contract wording is clear, succinct, and thorough. Avoid ambiguity or too sophisticated legal vocabulary.

•**Negotiate clauses**: If particular clauses in the contract are raising worries or problems, be open to discussion. A contract should be mutually agreed.

•**Review with Legal advice**: If it's a complex or high-value contract, consider having it evaluated by legal advice to guarantee legal compliance and protection.

•**Sign and Execute quickly**: Once the terms are agreed upon, quickly sign and execute the contract. Delays in execution might lead to difficulties.

•**Document All modifications**: If any modifications or amendments to the contract are made, ensure they are documented and signed by all parties concerned.

•**discuss Changes**: If conditions change throughout the contract time, discuss these changes quickly and work jointly to revise the contract if necessary.

•**Performance Metrics**: If applicable, create performance metrics and key performance indicators (KPIs) in the contract to monitor progress and success.

•**review and Improve**: After the contract is concluded, review the outcomes and experiences. Use this input to enhance future contracts and proposals.

The key to making contracts and proposals work is openness, mutual understanding, and a commitment to honoring the agreed-upon parameters. Effective communication and a willingness to adjust as circumstances change are key for successful contracts and proposals.

component of a successful proposal and agreement

Creating a good proposal and agreement involves attention to important components that explain expectations, duties, and conditions. Here are the basic aspects of a successful proposal and agreement:

1. **Introduction**: Begin with a clear and succinct introduction that sets the stage for what the proposal or agreement is about. Provide a brief description of the background and goal.

2.Objectives and Deliverables: Define the particular objectives and desired results of the project or agreement. Describe the deliverables that will be supplied, together with any milestones or dates.

3.Pricing and Payment Terms: Provide a full description of expenses, fees, or pricing structure. Specify the payment conditions, including the amount, due dates, and payment methods. Address any potential extra charges or contingencies.

4.schedule and Milestones: Include a project schedule with significant milestones and deadlines. This helps manage expectations and ensures all parties are aligned on the project's timeframe.

5.Terms and Conditions: Explicitly express the terms and conditions related to the proposal or agreement. This may involve problems like warranties, intellectual property rights, dispute resolution processes, or responsibility agreements.

6.Client's Responsibilities: Define the client's responsibilities and obligations in the project or agreement. Clarify what is expected of them, such as giving relevant information or approvals.

7.Templates and Legal Review: Consider utilizing templates or getting legal review, especially for complicated or high-value proposals and agreements, to guarantee legal compliance and protection.

Effective communication and mutual understanding are important to producing a successful proposal and agreement. Clearly identifying all these components helps ensure that all parties are on the same page, expectations are satisfied, and possible problems are minimized.

Conclusion

In conclusion, The Prosperity Mentor is not simply a book; it's your own guide to unlocking a world of financial prosperity and joy. Throughout these pages, you've gone on a transformational journey, delving deep into the art of thriving and mastering the attitude of abundance.

We've investigated the underlying concepts of wealth creation, built your individual prosperity blueprint, and uncovered the wisdom of mentors who have traveled the path of abundance before us. You've learned to make clear objectives and intentions that move you toward the life you picture, led by the force of your greatest desires.

But remember, the trip doesn't finish here. Your continual pursuit of success is a witness to your devotion to a life filled with purpose, riches, and well-being. Your dreams, your intentions, and your deeds are the keys to the endless possibilities that lay ahead.

As you bring the knowledge of this book into your everyday life, may you continue to make decisions that cultivate your prosperity, may your thinking stay unshakeable, and may you thrive in all facets of your existence. With resilience and a plethora of information at your disposal, there's no limit to the heights you may attain.

The actual power of The Prosperity Mentor resides in your hands. It's your path, your tale, and your legacy of success that you're constructing. So, embrace the chances, conquer the problems, and remember, the route to plenty is not only about riches; it's about living a life that resonates with your deepest aspirations.

As you stride into the future, may your days be filled with prosperity, your heart with appreciation, and your life with the irrefutable magic of flourishing. It's time to construct your own narrative of success and seize the life you've always dreamt of.

Your profitable path has only just begun, and with the direction of this mentor, your future is rich with possibilities.

Prosperity awaits. Embrace it.